Bouquets
AND Posies

GIFTS FROM NATURE

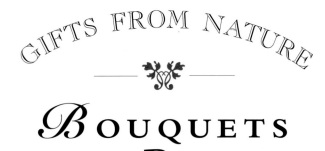

BOUQUETS AND POSIES

Beautiful floral arrangements for every occasion

BEVERLEY JOLLANDS

LORENZ BOOKS

First published in 1998 by Lorenz Books
an imprint of
Anness Publishing Limited
88-89 Blackfriars Road
London SE1 8HA

This edition published in the USA by Lorenz Books
Anness Publishing, Inc.,
27 West 20th Street, New York, NY 10011
(800) 354-9657

This edition distributed in Canada by Raincoast Books
8680 Cambie Street, Vancouver, V6P 6M9

ISBN 1 85967 587 5

A CIP catalogue record for this book is available from the British Library

Publisher: Joanna Lorenz
Project Editor: Joanne Rippin
Designers: Lisa Tai and Lilian Lindblom
Illustrations: Anna Koska

Printed and bound in Singapore

1 3 5 7 9 10 8 6 4 2

CONTENTS

INTRODUCTION

*I*t's always a pleasure to be given flowers, and it's really just as rewarding to give them or to choose them for yourself, whether you cut a few perfect, dewy blooms from your garden or select unusual treasures from a florist's stall. Arranging them into a lovely bouquet will make them a more special gift, and a greater pleasure for you.

Indispensable at weddings, and a delightful part of many other celebrations, bouquets and posies are a lovely way to say "Congratulations", "Happy birthday", "Thank you" or "Get well soon". This book presents a host of ideas for making the most of flowers without robbing them of their natural beauty and grace. There are also suggestions for turning dried flowers into beautiful and enduring arrangements.

Before you begin, sort all the material so that it is easily accessible. Clean the stems, stripping off thorns and any leaves that will be below the binding point – the point on the stems at which the finished arrangement is tied. For perfect proportions, this should be about two-thirds of the way down from the top of the bouquet. Arrange the focal flowers using an odd number of blooms: this will always produce a more balanced shape. Use the most fully open flowers towards the centre, framed by buds and smaller blooms.

Much smaller arrangements can be equally pleasing: a tiny scented posy makes a delightful gift, and is a wonderful way to present garden roses or fresh herbs. On an even smaller scale, elegant buttonholes, corsages and unusual decorations are included here to inspire you with new ways of using flowers.

BOUQUETS AND GIFTS

A bunch of freshly picked flowers is the most traditional and natural form of flower arrangement. The flowers can be arranged in the hand, creating a spiral effect by placing each stem at the same angle. This style of arrangement, known as the hand-tied or continental bouquet, is justifiably popular. Unlike more formal flat or sheaf bouquets, where all the stems are of differing lengths, the

hand-tied bouquet is ready to go into a vase without any further arrangement. Everyone loves to receive flowers: the time you spend arranging them will be the most valued part of your gift.

A SIMPLE GIFT OF ROSES

Sometimes a bunch of flowers fresh from the garden is the perfect small gift to cheer up a friend or to convey thanks. Arrange them prettily so that the recipient can simply unwrap the bouquet and put it straight into a vase.

- secateurs (pruning shears)
- garden roses
- eucalyptus stems
- scabious
- gilded brown paper
- ribbon

1 Using secateurs (pruning shears), cut each flower stem to approximately 15 cm/6 in long.

2 Gather the flowers together, surrounding each rose with some feathery eucalyptus, then adding the scabious.

3 Wrap the flowers in a square of gilded brown paper and tie with a pretty ribbon bow.

BLUE AND YELLOW SUMMER FLOWERS

The sunny yellow faces of sneezeweed become almost luminous when set against the electric blue of 'Blue Butterfly' delphiniums. This is a brave colour combination guaranteed to brighten anyone's day. The easy-to-make, hand-tied spiral bunch is designed to look as informal as possible.

- 10 stems 'Blue Butterfly' delphiniums
- 2 bunches sneezeweed
- (helenium)
- 3 stems dracaena
- raffia
- scissors

1 Sort the plant material and lay it out so that you can pick it up easily as you need it. Build the display by alternately adding stems of different flowers and foliage, while continuously turning the growing bunch in your hand.

2 Continue the process until all the materials are used and you have a balanced arrangement. Tie the bunch firmly at the binding point with raffia. Trim the stem ends level so that the bouquet can be put straight into a container.

RED TIED SHEAF

A tied sheaf of dried flowers arranged in the hand can be used as an attractive and informal wall decoration. The sheaf must be made with a flat back, but should have a profiled front to add visual interest. With such exotic colours, this display would work best in a richly coloured interior.

- large bunch dried lavender
- 10 stems *Protea compacta* buds
- 10 stems natural ti tree
- 15 stems dried red roses
- twine
- scissors
- wired satin ribbon

1 Lay out all the materials and separate the lavender stems into 10 smaller groups. Hold the longest *Protea* in your hand, and behind it add a slightly longer stem of ti tree, then hold slightly shorter rose stems to either side. Continue to add materials in a regular repeating sequence, spiralling the stems as you do so.

2 When all the materials have been used, tie the sheaf with twine at the binding point. Trim the stems so that they make up about one-third of the overall length of the sheaf.

3 To finish the display, tie the ribbon into a generous bow and attach it to the sheaf at the binding point.

PINK PEONY BOUQUET

This lovely bouquet uses deep pink roses and peonies and purple marjoram: modern preserving techniques mean that they are able to retain their strong natural colours. The bouquet is a loose, slightly domed arrangement that uses the flowers on long stems.

- 1 bunch dried marjoram
- 15 stems dried pink peonies
- 30 stems dried dark pink roses
- twine
- scissors
- ribbon

1 Lay out the materials so they are easily accessible and split the marjoram into 15 small bunches. Hold the first peony in your hand about two-thirds of the way down its stem. Add two roses, then a small bunch of marjoram and another peony, turning the bunch with every addition. Continue this sequence, occasionally varying your hand position to create a slightly domed shape.

2 When all the materials have been used, tie twine tightly around the binding point. Trim the stem ends evenly so that, below the binding point, they make up about one-third of the overall height of the bouquet. Finally, tie a ribbon around the binding point and finish in a bow.

SUMMER ROSE BUNDLE

This bright, compact arrangement would be a welcome gift for a sick friend at home or in hospital, with the advantage that a display this size will take very little precious bedside space.

- glue gun
- florist's dry foam disc, about 5 cm/ 2 in thick
- brown paper
- craft knife
- cutting mat
- stub (floral) wires
- pliers
- scissors

- 12 stems dried pink roses
- 1 bunch dried pink larkspur
- 3–4 cobra leaves or similar
- mossing (floral) pins
- raffia
- moss

1 Glue the florist's dry foam disc to the centre of a square of brown paper. Use a craft knife to make radiating cuts from the edge of the foam to the edge of the paper at roughly 1 cm/½ in intervals.

2 Fold up the paper strips to cover the foam. Twist a stub (floral) wire around the paper and the foam, making sure that all the paper strips are straight and neat at the base. Trim the paper in line with the top of the foam.

3 Prepare and cut the rose stems and larkspur, retaining as many of the leaves as possible. Starting in the centre, push the roses, one at a time, into the foam.

4 Add the larkspur around and between the roses. Fill any spaces with moss. Wrap three or four cobra leaves around the base, fixing each one in place with a mossing (floral) pin.

5 Twist a stub (floral) wire tightly around the leaves in line with the pins. Trim the leaves to make a stable base. Tie raffia around the base, to cover the fixings, and finish with a bow.

WEDDING BOUQUETS

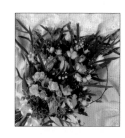

*M*aking a wedding bouquet for a friend or relative adds a lovely personal touch to her special day. Apart from the beauty of the flowers and the elegance of the design, the overall size of the bouquet is important. Wrap them securely in tape or ribbon to avoid any damage to clothes or hands. The projects in this chapter range from a simple bunch of dried roses to an ambitious and

formal arrangement in a traditional "shower" design. For those celebrating a long and happy marriage, there is an all-gold design to make as an anniversary gift.

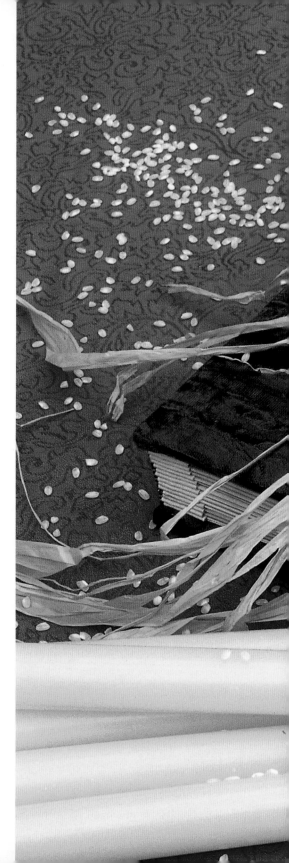

SPRING WEDDING FLOWERS

Springtime is a fitting season for making vows, when new spring buds are bursting forth with their promise of a glorious summer. This bouquet, in the traditional colours of spring, features tulips, anemones and feathery marguerites. It is composed of various "sections" grouped together to create an impression of abundance.

- variegated pittosporum
- sedum
- hebe
- eucalyptus
- 12 stems yellow tulips
- 12 stems marguerites

- 12 stems purple anemones
- 9 stems white spray roses
- twine
- scissors
- ribbon

1 Strip the lower leaves from the stems and lay out all the material. Take the first two pieces of foliage and cross them to begin the spiral. Build up the foliage base until the desired shape is achieved – the foliage should be quite dense.

2 Add the first group of flowers – the tulips – concentrating on one quarter of the bunch. Add the marguerites, anemones and roses in the remaining quarters. Tie the bouquet with twine at the binding point, cut the stems level and finish with a bow.

SIMPLE ROSE BOUQUET

The linear hand-tied bouquet is a very romantic arrangement, perfect for brides with long flowing dresses.
It may be held either pointing downwards or in the curve of an elbow. Yellow and white flowers are synonymous with spring,
and several branches of mimosa add a sharp, sweet fragrance to the bouquet.

- scissors
- 5 stems mimosa
- 5 stems 'Yellow Dot' spray roses
- 5 stems 'Tina' spray roses
- 5 stems pale yellow tulips
- 5 stems white tulips
- 5 stems white anemones
- variegated pittosporum
- variegated trailing ivy
- twine or raffia
- white or pale yellow ribbon

1 Strip all the stems of any leaves and thorns which would be below the binding point (about one-third of the way up each stem). Thorns should be neatly cut off so as not to damage the rose stems. Place a rose, a stem of mimosa and one of pittosporum in one hand to form the bouquet's centre.

2 Lay each subsequent stem at an angle of 45°, always in the same direction. Turn the bouquet in the hand to develop the spiral shape. Hold the stems quite firmly at the binding point while adding new flowers.

3 Twist the twine or raffia just above the hand and tie firmly at the binding point. Trim all the stems to an even length and finish the bouquet with a bow.

BRIDAL SHOWER BOUQUET

The danger with some wired shower bouquets is that the wiring can dominate the display, giving a stiff, formal feel to the whole arrangement. The problem has been overcome here by wiring the blooms and greenery halfway down their natural stems, which allows more natural movement in the spray.

- long stems of ruscus
- trailing ivy
- eucalyptus
- 24 stems 'Oceana' roses
- 5 stems 'Casablanca' lilies
- fatsia leaves

- scissors
- stub (floral) wires
- florist's (stem-wrap) tape
- florist's reel wire
- ribbon

1 Lay out the flowers roughly in the shape required, making sure they have long enough stems to form the cascade effect. Wire all the stems with one or more stub (floral) wires to achieve the required lengths. Tape all the wired stems. Take the longest stem of ruscus and bend the wire leg right back, to form the handle. The point at which the wire is bent is the binding point: attach the florist's reel wire here.

2 Add shorter stems of foliage on either side, graduating each piece carefully to make a V-shape. Bind each stem into position with the reel wire. Work in front of a mirror so that you can see the shape you are building. Add the first and longest rose stem on top of the first ruscus stem. This rose should also be the most tightly closed.

3 Introduce the roses on either side at approriate intervals, as with the foliage, until you reach the widest point of the bouquet. Place the most open roses nearest to the binding point. Insert the lilies with the buds forming the longest points and the most open flowers around the binding point to create a focus.

4 Begin the top of the bouquet by binding a stem of ruscus to achieve the total length of the spray. Place more foliage on both sides, beginning at the top and working towards the centre and checking the outline as you go. Place the fatsia leaves at the back to provide support and definition. Bind in the central material, making sure the central lily and rose are placed in vertically.

5 Cut and taper the stems to form the handle and bind with reel wire. Wrap the handle with ribbon and finish with a bow near the binding point.

TRAILING LILY BOUQUET

This classic "shower" bouquet has a generous trailing shape and incorporates white lilies as its focal flowers, using the traditional, fresh bridal colour combination of white, cream and green. As the flowers are not wired, the arrangement has a natural, loose appearance, with long stems of euphorbia and asters emphasizing the flowing shape.

- 10 stems *Lilium longiflorum*
- 10 stems cream *Eustoma grandiflorum*
- 10 stems white *Euphorbia fulgens*
- 5 stems moluccella
- 10 stems white asters 'Monte Cassino'
- flowering dill
- trailing ivy
- twine
- scissors
- raffia

1 Lay out all the materials so that they are easily accessible. Hold one stem of lilies in your hand about 25 cm/10 in down from its flower head. Add the other flowers and trails of ivy in a regular sequence to get an even distribution of materials throughout the bouquet. As you do this, keep turning the bunch in your hand to make the stems form a spiral.

2 To one side of the bouquet add materials on longer stems than the central flower – these will form the trailing element of the display. To the opposite side add slightly shorter stems to become the top of the bouquet.

3 When you have finished the bouquet, tie it firmly with twine at the binding point. Cut the stems evenly, about 13 cm/5 in below the binding point.

4 Tie raffia around the binding point and form a bow that sits on top of the stems, facing upwards towards the person carrying the bouquet.

GOLDEN WEDDING BOUQUET

This shimmering bouquet makes an unequivocal Golden Wedding statement. Unashamed in its use of yellows and golds, the colours are carried right through the design in the flowers, the wrapping paper, the binding twine and the ribbon, even to a fine sprinkling of gold dust.

- 20 stems golden yellow ranunculus
- 20 stems mimosa
- gold twine
- scissors
- 2 sheets gold-

coloured tissue paper in 2 shades
- strip of gold fabric 45 x 15 cm/ 18 x 6 in
- gold dust glitter

1 Clean the stems of ranunculus and mimosa from about one-third of the way down and lay them out so that they are easily accessible. Holding a stem of ranunculus in your hand, start to build the bouquet by adding alternate stems of mimosa and ranunculus, turning the flowers in your hand all the time so that the stems form a spiral.

2 When all the flowers have been arranged in your hand, tie the stems together at the binding point with the gold twine. When secured, trim the stems to a length approximately one-third of the overall height of the bouquet.

Arrange white flowers with grey foliage for a silver wedding gift or dark red flowers with copper leaves for a ruby wedding.

3 To wrap the bouquet, lay the two sheets of tissue on top of each other and lay the bouquet diagonally on top. Pull up the sides of the paper, then the front, and hold these in place by tying gold twine around the binding point. To complete the bouquet, tie the strip of gold fabric around the binding point and create a bow. Scatter a little gold dust over the flowers. Separate the sheets of tissue to give a fuller appearance.

DRIED WEDDING POSY

*The great advantage of using dried materials for a wedding is that what you are making can be prepared well in advance.
This posy is a mixture of only two types of flower, but any combination can be used to produce a wonderful effect. Always bear in mind
that the posy will be carried for some time, and that too much material will make it large and uncomfortable to hold.*

- 2 bunches dried
  pink roses
- 2 bunches dried
  pink larkspur
- stub (floral) wire

- pliers
- scissors or
  secateurs (pruning
  shears)
- raffia

Make sure that some of the flowers have interest down the stems and not just at the top: the side of the posy is as important as the top surface and is likely to be seen as much.

1 Open and separate the bunches, making two piles of the flowers. Arrange the flowers in your hand, alternating the two varieties and turning the bunch as you add more flowers to produce a small circular arrangement.

2 Wrap a stub (floral) wire around the stems at the binding point and twist the two ends together to hold the posy in shape.

3 Trim the stems evenly, leaving them long enough below the binding point to be held in the hand comfortably.

4 Tie the posy with plenty of raffia to cover the stub wire and give a comfortable grip.

POSIES AND TUSSIE MUSSIES

Simple, hand-tied posies are a very special gift, and their diminutive size implies an intimacy that makes them personal and unique. The smaller the posy, the tinier and more delicate the flowers and foliage need to be, with wispy, frond-like leaves defining the shape of individual flower heads. Full of fresh herbs and flowers, tussie mussies were carried from the sixteenth century to ward off illness

and disguise unpleasant smells, and ladies carried them as a form of personal perfume. Some of the tussie mussies in this chapter follow the traditional design, while others are more original.

GARDEN ROSE POSY

A small posy is a delightful way to present garden roses, especially old varieties whose stems may be short or wayward. Remove all the thorns carefully before you begin. A box covered in wrapping paper both protects the flowers and offers an element of surprise, and wrapping a little moistened tissue around the stem ends will keep the flowers fresh for several hours.

- about 12 stems roses
- raffia
- secateurs (pruning shears)

- ribbon
- scissors

1 Arrange the roses in a tight posy, bind with raffia and trim the stems. Leaving enough ribbon to tie a bow, start winding the ribbon from the binding point.

2 When you reach the bottom, tuck the ribbon over the base of the stems and then wind it back up to the top.

3 When you reach the starting point, tie the ribbon in a knot before adding a bow. Cut the ribbon ends on a slant to stop them fraying.

MIDSUMMER NOSEGAY

*Make a beautifully scented nosegay full of the freshness of a summer garden. The glorious damask rose used here is
'Rosa Mundi'. Sweet peas are included for their intoxicating fragrance, while the softly frilled edging of lady's mantle leaves
makes a protective circle around the posy.*

- large damask rose
  'Rosa Mundi'
- 5 flower heads
  lady's mantle
  (*Alchemilla mollis*)
- and 19 leaves
- 17 stems sweet peas
- scissors
- florist's (stem-wrap)
  tape

1 Hold the rose in one hand and gradually surround it with the lady's mantle flowers, then with the sweet peas, turning the posy as you work to form a neat circle.

2 Add the lady's mantle leaves to form a frill around the flowers. Trim all the stems to an even length and bind them together with florist's (stem-wrap) tape.

FRESH HERBS POSY

There is a long-established tradition of taking a bunch of flowers as a gift when visiting friends, but a posy of home-grown herbs is a more unusual, and very attractive, alternative, which makes a useful present.

- selection of freshly picked herbs
- bucket
- twine
- scissors
- ribbon

1 Condition the herbs by standing them in deep water in a bucket for at least 3 hours before making the posy. Spread all the herbs out in groups on the work surface before you begin to arrange them. Assemble the posy, holding it loosely in one hand and adding and adjusting each stem with the other.

2 When you are finally happy with the arrangement, tie the bunch firmly at the binding point with twine.

3 Trim the ends of the stems level and decorate the posy with a ribbon tied in a bow.

The herbs should be picked early in the day and stood in deep water in a cool place to condition them before making the posy. This will ensure that they still look fresh and appetizing when they arrive at their destination.

LAVENDER TUSSIE MUSSIE

The scent of fresh lavender is particularly soothing, and this bunch will dry beautifully and go on giving pleasure for ages.
If you are lucky enough to find white lavender, or if you grow it in your garden, it makes a delightful tussie mussie
when contrasted with the more conventional blue.

- 1 bunch deep blue lavender
- 1 bunch white lavender
- raffia, twine or elastic band
- secateurs (pruning shears)
- ribbon

1 Arrange a circle of blue lavender stems around a small bunch of the stems of white lavender. Secure with a piece of raffia, twine or an elastic band.

2 Arrange the remaining white lavender around the blue and secure the complete bunch with raffia, twine or an elastic band. Trim the stalks to a even length.

3 Complete the arrangement by tying a length of wide ribbon around the posy to cover the binding. Tie it in a generous, decorative bow.

FRESH HERBS TUSSIE MUSSIE

An aromatic posy makes a lovely scented gift or can be used as a table centre. This tussie mussie is made from chive flowers, rosemary and comfrey: the blue and purple tones of the chive and comfrey flowers are perfectly offset by the rich green of the fragrant rosemary leaves.

- 5 stems chive flowers
- bunch of rosemary
- raffia
- secateurs (pruning shears)

- bunch of comfrey (*Symphytum caucasicum*)
- grosgrain ribbon

1 Arrange the chive flowers in a bunch and make a circle of rosemary stems around them. Tie with raffia and trim the stems.

2 In the same way, add a ring of comfrey, tie it in place and trim the stems.

3 Add a final ring of rosemary, tie in position with raffia and trim to an even length. Finish with a length of grosgrain ribbon tied into a bow.

BLUE AND WHITE TUSSIE MUSSIES

These two small arrangements use delicate flowers massed together.

For the white tussie mussie:
• 1 stem dracaena
• 9 small stems blackberries
• 9 white Japanese anemones
• twine
• ribbon
• scissors

For the blue tussie mussie:
• 4–5 stems 'Blue Butterfly' delphiniums
• 3 stems rosehips
• 5 small Virginia creeper leaves
• twine
• ribbon
• scissors

1 Start with a central flower and add stems of foliage and flowers, turning the posy in your hand to build the design into a spiral.

2 Once all the ingredients have been used and the bunch is complete, tie it firmly at the binding point with twine. Make the second tussie mussie in the same way.

3 Trim the ends of the flower stems to an even length. Finish with ribbon bows.

OLD–FASHIONED ROSE POSY

This hand-tied posy combines the velvet beauty of blown red and apricot roses with the fresh scent of mint.
Finished with a natural raffia bow, the posy has a fresh, just-gathered look.

- 5 stems red and 5 stems pale apricot roses
- secateurs (pruning shears)
- 20 stems flowering mint
- 6 vine leaves
- twine
- raffia

1 Remove all the thorns and the lower leaves from the rose stems. Starting with a rose in one hand, add alternately two stems of mint and one rose stem until all the materials are used. Keep turning the posy as you build to form the stems into a spiral. Finally, add the vine leaves to form an edging to the arrangement, and tie with twine at the binding point.

2 Trim the ends of the stems so that they form approximately one-third of the overall height of the posy. Tie raffia around the binding point and form it into a secure bow.

VICTORIAN POSY

The traditional Victorian posy took the form of a series of concentric circles of flowers. Each circle contained just one type of flower, with variations only from one circle to the next. Such strict geometry produces very formal arrangements, which are particularly well suited to dried flowers.

- scissors
- 11 stems dried white roses
- 18 stems dried pink roses
- 3 stems dried pink peonies
- stub (floral) wires
- 12 stems glycerined eucalyptus
- 2 bunches phalaris grass

- 1 bunch dried honesty
- 1 bunch dried linseed
- 10 small clusters dried hydrangea
- florist's (stem-wrap) tape
- florist's reel wire
- ribbon

1 Cut the roses and peonies to a stem length of 3 cm/1¼ in and mount them individually on stub (floral) wires. Cut the eucalyptus stems to 10 cm/4 in and remove the leaves from the bottom 3 cm/1¼ in, then wire. Wire the phalaris grass and honesty heads in groups of five and mount the groups on stub (floral) wires to extend their stem lengths to 25 cm/10 in. Repeat with groups of linseed and hydrangea. Bind all the wired elements with florist's (stem-wrap) tape.

2 Hold the central flower, a single white rose, in your hand and arrange the three peony heads around it, then bind together with florist's reel wire, starting 10 cm/ 4 in down the extended stems.

3 Rotating the growing posy in your hand, form a circle of pink rose heads around the peonies and bind this to the main stem. Around this, form another circle, this time alternating white rose heads and clusters of hydrangea, and bind. Each additional circle of flower heads will be at an increasing angle to the central flower, to create a domed shape.

4 Next add a circle of phalaris grass to the posy, followed by a circle of alternating honesty heads and linseed. Bind each circle when complete with florist's reel wire at the binding point.

5 Finally, bind on a circle of eucalyptus so that the leaves form a border to the posy and cover any exposed wires underneath. To form a handle, trim off any excess wires and tape the bundle of bound wires. Cover the handle with ribbon.

ROSE AND LAVENDER POSY

A bunch of carefully selected and beautifully arranged dried flowers will long outlast fresh blooms, to become an enduring reminder of a happy occasion. The language of flowers interprets lavender as "devoted attention" and pink roses as symbols of affection, so this posy should really only be made for a very special friend.

- stub (floral) wires
- 12 large glycerined leaves
- florist's (stem-wrap) tape
- large bunch dried

- lavender
- 12 stems dried rosebuds
- florist's reel wire
- scissors
- paper ribbon

1 Fold a stub (floral) wire to form a 15 cm/6 in stalk. Attach a leaf to the top by its stem and bind in place using florist's (stem-wrap) tape, pulling and wrapping the tape down to the end of the wire. Repeat the process to wire 12 leaves.

2 Divide the lavender into several small bunches. Hold them together loosely, setting the bunches at different angles to give a good shape. This will form the basic structure of the posy.

3 Taking a single rosebud at a time, push the stems into the lavender, spacing them out evenly around the posy.

4 Bind the bunch of lavender and roses with florist's reel wire so it will keep its shape while you work. Trim the stems evenly, then edge the posy with the wire-mounted leaves. Bind in place again.

5 Unravel the paper ribbon and use to bind all the stems together tightly, covering them and the wires completely. Tie the ends of the ribbon into a bow.

DRIED FLOWER TUSSIE MUSSIES

These tussie mussies are made of small spiralled bunches of lavender-scented dried flowers and have a rich medieval look.

For the red rose tussie mussie:
- scissors
- 20 stems dried red roses
- 1 bunch dried love-in-a-mist (nigella)
- 1 bunch dried lavender
- twine
- ribbon

For the pink rose tussie mussie:
- scissors
- 20 stems dried pink roses
- small bunch love-in-a-mist (nigella) seed heads
- small bunch dried lavender
- small bunch phalaris
- twine
- ribbon

1 To make either tussie mussie, cut all the materials to a stem length of approximately 18 cm/ 7 in. Set them all out in separate groups for easy access. Start by holding a single rose in your hand and add the other materials one by one.

2 Add, in turn, stems of love-in-a-mist, lavender, rose and phalaris (if using) to the central stem. Continue this sequence, all the while turning the bunch in your hand to ensure that the stems form a spiral.

3 Hold the growing bunch about two-thirds of the way down the stems. When all the materials are in place, secure the bunch by tying twine around the binding point of the stems. Trim the bottoms of the stems evenly. Tie a ribbon around the binding point.

DRIED HERBAL POSY

This pretty posy, edged with a traditional cotton frill, would make a very pretty and long-lasting dressing table decoration.
Dried red roses are delicately offset by a cloud of subtly coloured alchemilla and marjoram flowers.

- small bunch dried red roses
- florist's reel wire
- small bunch dried alchemilla
- small bunch dried marjoram
- scissors
- cotton posy frill in deep pink
- 3 sprays dried bay leaves
- glue gun
- florist's (stem wrap) tape
- ribbon

1 Start with a small cluster of red roses, binding them with florist's reel wire to form the centre. Surround the roses with a circle of alchemilla. Bind in some marjoram, then more red roses and alchemilla, until you are happy with the size of the posy. Trim the stems evenly and push them through the centre of the posy frill.

2 Separate the bay leaves from the stems and glue them into the posy one at a time, through the arrangement and around the edge as a border. Push the posy frill up to the flowers and fasten with florist's (stem-wrap) tape. Tie a length of ribbon around the stems and finish with a bow.

CORSAGES, BUTTONHOLES AND DECORATIONS

It used to be the fashion for gentlemen to present their ladies with an elaborate corsage of scented flowers to wear on a special occasion such as a grand ball. This custom is now restricted to weddings, but it is quite possible to create some really attractive arrangements for both men and women to wear on formal occasions. Traditional etiquette demands that ladies wear corsages with

the flowers pointing downwards and gentlemen wear buttonholes with the flowers upright. These tiny arrangements can provide the perfect finishing touches to a special gift or as part of a table setting.

GENTLEMAN'S BUTTONHOLE AND LADY'S CORSAGE

These two designs combine roses with more unusual elements such as sea holly and berries to create original and beautiful ornaments.

For the gentleman's buttonhole:

- 1 stem 'Ecstasy' rose
- scissors
- stub (floral) wire
- florist's (stem-wrap) tape
- 3 heads eryngium (sea holly)
- 3 heads lavender
- florist's reel wire
- 3 ivy leaves

For the lady's corsage:

- stub (floral) wires
- 2 stems 'First Red' roses
- 3 ivy leaves, 2 large and 1 smaller
- florist's reel wire
- florist's (stem-wrap) tape
- scissors
- 2 sprigs cotoneaster berries
- co-ordinating wired ribbon

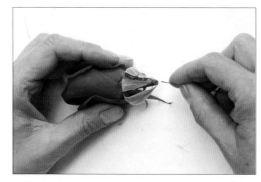

1 To make the gentleman's buttonhole, cut the stem off the rose about 1 cm/½ in below the flower head. Push a stub (floral) wire through the remaining stem and up into the head.

2 Bind florist's (stem-wrap) tape around the stem and wire, sealing them together securely. Tape the eryngium stems and the lavender heads to create two little bunches.

3 Thread a length of florist's reel wire through the main vein at the back of each ivy leaf, leaving a long end of wire. Hold the shorter end of the wire down the back of the stem and wind the longer end around both stem and wire, then tape the stem.

4 Arrange the flowers with the ivy leaves behind them creating a flat back to the buttonhole. Tape all the stems together.

5 To make the lady's corsage, wire the roses and ivy leaves as for the buttonhole.

6 Group the roses and berries, using the ivy leaves as the flat back for the corsage, and bind the stems together. Finish with a ribbon bow.

CLASSIC ROSE CORSAGE

Cream roses make a classically elegant corsage, beautifully set off by the cool, understated greens of the supporting foliage: ivy, eucalyptus and the leaves of the roses themselves.

- 3 stems 'Oceana' roses
- stub (floral) wires
- florist's (stem-wrap) tape
- rose leaves

- ivy leaves
- eucalyptus
- scissors
- florist's reel wire

1 Wire each rose individually with a stub (floral) wire and bind with florist's (stem-wrap) tape. Wire and tape each piece of foliage, using florist's reel wire. Take a stub (floral) wire and attach the first rose leaf to the end of it, securing it with tape.

2 Add an ivy leaf on either side of the first rose leaf, then add the first rose.

3 Introduce two more rose leaves vertically, at opposite ends, and place the focal rose between them, also vertically. Fill in any holes between the roses with clusters of eucalyptus.

4 Place the final rose at a diagonal to the focal rose, framing it with two ivy leaves at opposite ends. Add a final rose leaf at the end of the spray. Trim the wire and bind with tape.

POSY BUTTONHOLES

*These tiny versions of a Victorian lace-frilled posy are quite easy to make and can be worn as an unusual buttonhole or corsage.
Surround the central flower with herbs or scented leaves to make an original and fragrant decoration. Tiny posy frills are available from
specialist floral suppliers, or you can make your own version by cutting out the centre of a paper doily.*

- 1 medium-sized
  flower
- sprigs of fresh
  herbs
- stub (floral) wire

- scissors
- miniature posy frill
  or trimmed doily
- florist's (stem-wrap)
  tape

1 Use a single flower such as a rose as the centrepiece for the arrangement. Wrap the sprigs of herb foliage – such as parsley – around it and bind tightly with wire.

2 Push the stems through the centre of the frill. Trim them to a suitable length for a buttonhole and wrap them completely with florist's (stem-wrap) tape.

A small spray carnation would be a very effective centrepiece instead of a rose. Try using variegated scented geranium leaves, or rosemary, sage, lavender or box.

AUTUMN CORSAGE

A contrasting cluster of orange and blue makes this sweet-smelling corsage a perfect finishing touch. Adapt the materials as necessary to match the colours of individual outfits.

- rosehips
- scissors
- stub (floral) wires
- florist's (stem-wrap) tape
- ivy leaves
- marjoram
- rowanberries

- bottlebrush
- sorrel
- rosemary
- moluccella
- mint
- blue thistle

1 Cut the rosehip stems to 2.5 cm/1 in and mount them on stub (floral) wires, binding with florist's (stem-wrap) tape to secure. Wire the foliage as necessary. The ivy leaves should be individually wire-stitched, and delicate stems, such as the marjoram and rowanberries, should be wired in bunches. Tape all the wired stems.

2 Choose the smallest flower heads and the smallest ivy leaves to begin the spray. Gradually introduce larger heads and leaves. Tape each new addition to the previous one to secure it, trimming excess wires as you go.

3 The binding point is positioned behind the focal group of rosehips, the widest and highest point of the spray. The binding tape should not change position from this point.

4 The remainder of the spray is half the length of the first section. Build up the elements to meet the central group. Cut the excess wires to about 2.5–4 cm/1–1½ in below the binding point at the centre. Taper them to make a slender false stem and cover it with tape.

GIFT WRAP WITH DRIED FLOWERS

❧

To make a present extra special, why not make the wrapping part of the gift? This decoration is constructed like a dried flower corsage and is bound to be kept as a memento of your thoughtfulness.

- 1 dried sunflower
- scissors
- 1 dried pomegranate
- stub (floral) wires
- 3 dried fungi pieces

- 3 dried orange slices
- florist's (stem-wrap) tape
- florist's reel wire
- raffia
- gift-wrapped box

1 Cut the sunflower to a stem length of 2.5 cm/1 in and mount it and the pomegranate on stub (floral) wires. Wire the fungi and orange slices.

2 Wrap all the wired materials with tape, then attach the three orange slices to one side of the sunflower and pomegranate, and the three layers of fungi on the other side. Bind all these in place using florist's reel wire.

3 Trim the wire stems to a length of 5 cm/2 in and tape together with florist's (stem-wrap) tape. Tie the raffia around the present and push the wired stem of the decoration under the raffia knot. Secure in place with a stub wire.

SPRING NAPKIN DECORATIONS

The sophisticated gold and white colour combination used in these elegant and delicate napkin decorations would be perfect for a formal dinner or an important occasion such as a wedding. In addition to its exquisite scent, the tiny bells of lily-of-the-valley visually harmonize with the pure white of the cyclamen.

For each napkin:
- sprig of small-leaved ivy
- scissors
- 4–5 stems lily-of-the-valley
- 3 stems dwarf cyclamen (*Cyclamen persicum*)
- 3 cyclamen leaves
- gold cord

1 Fold each napkin into a rectangle, then roll it into a cylindrical shape. Wrap an ivy sprig around the middle of the napkin. Tie the stem firmly in a knot.

2 Take the lily-of-the-valley and cyclamen flowers and create a small sheaf in your hand by spiralling the stems. Place one cyclamen leaf at the back of the flowers for support, and two more around the cyclamen flowers to emphasize the focal point. Tie at the binding point with gold cord. Lay the flat back of the sheaf on top of the napkin and ivy, and wrap the excess gold cord around the napkin, gently tying it into a bow on top of the stems.

FRAGRANT HERBAL NAPKIN TIES

This beautiful alternative to a napkin ring is easy to make and very effective: simply use any reasonably sturdy trailing foliage to bind the napkin and then create a focal point by adding leaves, berries or flower heads of your choice. You can adapt this idea to many different occasions by using different types of flowers and herbs.

For each napkin:
- scissors
- long, thin, flexible
  rosemary stem

- 3 lemon geranium leaves
- 2 or 3 heads flowering mint

1 Find a suitable stem of rosemary, long and flexible enough to wrap around the rolled napkin once or twice. Tie the stem securely.

2 Arrange the lemon geranium leaves and the mint flower heads by gently pushing their stems through the knot of the binding rosemary stem.

INDEX